SIC

David Salle

17 September to 11 October 2003

Waddington Galleries

David Salle's Virtual Realities

by Robert Rosenblum

Important artists have a way of providing two-way mirrors for the world we live in. I thought about this while watching TV and wondering, at the same time, how I would begin these remarks on David Salle's latest work. Looking at the screen, I gradually began to think I was looking at one of his paintings. Here was something that clearly resembled the real world, but just as clearly looked like a synthetic facsimile of it; and here was a way of seeing this cloned universe by packaging it into tidy squares and rectangles, sometimes side by side as in split screen images, sometimes in more complex geometric tiers or overlays. Moreover, the virtual realities we see within these artificial boundaries are always fragmentary and deceptive, each momentary illusion instantly cancelled by its neighbour. Each partial image, in fact, is flush against the other, seesawing between a flat geometric format on the screen and the ephemeral *trompe l'oeil* of something borrowed from the world around us. And the tempo of change, far more than in any movie, is bewilderingly rapid and unpredictable. Whether from the interruptions of commercials and news breaks, or the discontinuities of channel surfing and jump cuts, everything moves at an electronic pace, with a frenzied mix of people, objects, and patterns juggled non-stop before one's eyes. Any old-fashioned sense of major and minor, central and peripheral, present and past is gone. And the once measurable distinctions between near and far, large and small have become no less obsolete. Isn't this the way of seeing that Salle had finally mastered in the 1980s and that might almost be a manifesto of a generation nurtured on the rectangular screen world of movies, video cameras, computers and, above all, TV?

If TV now seems to reflect what Salle's paintings look like, his paintings return the compliment, sorting out and refining on an aesthetic tightrope the endless visual barrage we live in. As for the current group of a dozen paintings, my art historian's curiosity kept being tweaked by passing fragments that I could, couldn't, or could almost recognise. A few were clear. For instance, there were the sizeable details of two Manet still-lifes of 1866, one with half a poached salmon (*150 Degrees*), the other with peaches and grapes (*Evaporation Machine*). But the easy identification of these paintings is set askew by the odd croppings Salle further imposed upon images whose visual fields, typically for Manet, were already fragmentary. The edibles, fruit and fish, were now framed by a square, not a horizontal format, which zoomed in on the centrepiece of the still-life display but completely undermined the more stable original context of a table setting in a room. They looked, in fact, like stills snatched from a film about art, in which a roving camera pauses for a moment on one detail of a painting and immediately goes on to another. And then, there is the disturbing fact that, as in the illusory surfaces of a photograph, these replicas of Manet's paintings, even though hand-painted, seem to have wilfully overlooked the master's succulent handling of pigment, substituting a completely inert and impersonal paint surface that makes us realise we are looking at the image of an image.

In another still-life quotation here, at the top of *Spill*, the distance from the original has accrued even more layers. A completely flat and regular pattern of grey (a non-colour that couldn't be more at odds with the organic hues of still-life painting) offers a contradictory support for the modelled reds, oranges, and yellows of the seven apples left floating above it with nothing left to explain the shadows they cast. Where does this brief quote come from? The museum-going eye might at first match it with some apples stolen from a table top by Cézanne or perhaps by Courbet; but in fact, this fragment of rounded organic forms has been excerpted from a painting by de Chirico. And that ups the ante, since it is taken from one of the later de Chiricos in which this master of retrospection is self-consciously imitating passages from nineteenth-century paintings, recycling them in his own new translations. When Salle, in turn, recycles de Chirico, this palimpsest of historical images becomes still more dense. What at first look like some homeless apples echo through the corridors of modern painting and then, forced to hover above a flat heraldic shape, become not a still-life painting, but rather an abstract logo that stands for a still-life painting.

Looking to the right of this emblem, another hybrid is captured in Salle's historical view-finder, this time a female nude, or rather the remnants of one, since, as in so many antique sculptures, her vigorous young body is missing both head and arms. And given the abrupt cropping at the waist, we can only guess whether the lower parts of her body are damaged or not. A fragment of a fragment, it seems to be at once modern and ancient, and also fuses the illusions offered by drawing and sculpture. Is this a painted image of an actual sculpture or is this a painted image of a drawing that imitates sculpture? Moreover, it morphs the history of sculpture, slipping from memories of classical nudes, ravaged by time, into the world of modern sculpture so often quoted by Salle, here evoking the ghosts of Rodin's marble and bronze resurrections of headless, limbless classical bodies. But from these high-art sources, this nude then moves into twentieth-century visual vernacular. Like diagrams in how-to books for beginning artists, its illusion of modelled flesh is rendered in the most mechanical, unsexy patterns of broadly schematic planes and shadows, an anonymous, elementary vocabulary that Salle has used since the 1980s to render the female body, either nude or partly undressed. And to undermine further any hierarchies of true and false, past and present, great or ordinary, Salle juxtaposes these more contemporary nudes with quotations from the history of modern figure sculpture. In *Spill*, Lehmbruck's flailing male nude, a famous bronze, is seen in its entirety, paired, though on a totally different scale, with Salle's mutilated but robust female torso. And in *Passers-by*, a similar yes and no is offered by the close proximity of a complete view of another bronze reduced to miniaturist size, a female nude by Degas who complements an overtly contemporary torso, a woman from our own world who wears a white bra but whose head and limbs are absent, thanks not to the weathering of history, but to the artist's surprising cropping at top, sides, and bottom.

One of the most distinctive features of Salle's work, in fact, is this fascination with the strange visual products that result from framing people and things in unexpected ways, all the more disturbing insofar as what we see seems as accidental as a photo taken by an amateur who was unaware that the sitter's head had slipped outside the camera's field of vision. Salle's women (who, like Degas's, are often dancers or nudes at their toilette) almost never appear as complete bodies, but are captured instead as unidentifiable torsos in rectangular cages. The occasional male may fare better, as in the snapshot figure framed by two semi-nudes in *Passers-by*; but in the case of a would-be portrait, *Massimo with Daffodils*, even a male sitter (the New York art dealer Massimo Audiello) is beheaded by the unyielding tyranny of the framing, his identity left only in half of the title and further threatened by the fact that what remains of him has to compete with an overlay of two daffodils, the kind of superposition that offers another of Salle's many nods in the direction of the later Picabia. Such a shuffle between still-life and figure painting is, in fact, common in these works, which constantly treat flowers, fruit and flesh as arbitrary components of a blatantly artificial whole, a new kind of photomontage. So it is that in *Passers-by*, the three fragmented figures below are matched above by a trio of white orchids floating on a camouflage-like pattern that might have been chosen from a book of wallpaper samples. Similarly, in *Moraine*, a trio of headless nudes below is echoed in the upper tier by a regimented selection of flowers and modern pottery displayed like trophies against another flat pattern of abstract coloured bands.

To many eyes and imaginations, there is much food here for psychosexual interpretations; and even grist for more combative feminist mills. Salle's occasional marriage of flowers and female sexuality is, to be sure, an ancient theme and one explored in countless variations by both male and female artists (as in Georgia O'Keeffe's almost gynaecological close-ups of flowers). But more conspicuous and, to many, more troubling is the way that Salle's treatment of the female body deprives it totally of intelligence and individuality, often leaving nothing but a torso to trigger erotic responses. Nevertheless, this, too, perpetuates traditions that, dating back to the maimed fragments of classical Venuses, were revived in unexpectedly new translations in the last century and a half, in both painting and sculpture, as well as photography. Think of Courbet, Degas, Rodin, Maillol, Weston, Pearlstein, not to mention a woman painter who specialises in truncated female bodies, Jenny Saville. However, the particular way Salle reincarnates the female nude is something else, essentially no different from his treatment of any object, animate or inanimate, that he chooses to include in his pictorial scrapbook, whether an old-master painting, a pitcher from the 1950s, or a collection of men's hats. In his hands, the entire world, whether flesh or paint or pottery, becomes strangely depersonalised and texture-less, transformed into remote replicas no longer capable of producing the immediate responses we would have to the real thing. For instance, the potential sexual charge in Salle's nudes is defused by his own coldly matter-of-fact manner of painting and cropping, leaving the female body as anatomically schematic and lifeless as an undressed mannequin in a department-store window. For Salle, all images are mute ciphers to be played with in his pictorial chess games. So it is that the potential Romantic thrill of an ostensibly awesome vista of white icebergs reflected in a blue sea (*Spill*) is instantly erased by a rendering so schematic, scale-less and detached that we might as well be looking at small mineral samples laid out on a blue-glass coffee table. In *Evaporation Machine*, the upper tier baffles our reflexes in a similar way, offering a would-be perspective view of the corner of an empty room that refuses to maintain its clearly diagrammed illusion. And within this contradictory space, two leafy, flowering plants, totally out of scale and restlessly shifting from flat decorative patterns to free-standing branches, also refuse to register as traditional pictorial fictions. (There may be clues to this unsettling, antiseptic interior in some of de Chirico's late fantasies of rooms rendered in dry perspective and occupied by almost palpable silhouettes and cut-outs of a radiant sun.) And to return to the Manet quote in *150 Degrees*, the exposed pink flesh of the salmon on a platter has become as inedible and artificial as the three lemons in *Lemon Tree*, much as the upper tier of the painting, with its roof-top and palm-tree view of Venice, California, seen against the leafy silhouette of an artificial flower, is transformed into a decorative network of geometric patterns in which the sun could no more shine than it could in one of the Rococo pastoral landscapes that Salle has often quoted from *toile de Jouy* textile and wallpaper designs.

Salle's grasp of that virtual reality which stealthily usurps our old-fashioned sense of what is real gives a special spin here to two smaller paintings in this group, one of daffodils, the other of tulips. Although they might be conventionally categorised as still-life paintings, they seem, like the female nudes or the Manets, to have had their vital juices extracted from them. And given the fact that they are seen as single images, their difference from traditional flower-painting becomes even more apparent, hovering as they do between enlarged reproductions of an existing image of flowers and a decorative component that might be used, say, for wallpaper or china or a cake decoration. And gradually, we understand what Salle means when he says that if you repaint something, it is a new thing - it's not a reproduction; it's something else.[1] In this, he is like the inventor of a new vocabulary in which commonplaces are translated into a new language that is deceptively similar to those we knew, but that gradually become more and more distant from the originals. What at first may look like part of a Manet or a piece of pottery gradually becomes something quite different, as we learn to measure more subtly the gulf that separates originals and facsimiles. So it is that the simplest of his flower paintings turn into something as odd as science-fiction, curious clones for a new age in which the inherited concepts of still-life painting become anachronisms from an ever more distant era.

But more typically, Salle thrives not so much on single images as on the more complex balancing act of giving equal time to totally disparate things, to a world in which a man's hat has no more pictorial or emotional weight than a woman's torso. The wonder is that these collisions end up looking inevitable, making us feel that only *this* Degas bronze would work with *these* white orchids or that only *this* china dish could complete a triptych which gives the same visual importance to a close-up of three lemons and then, to a close-up of a woman's face. In this, Salle seems to be inventing a new system of grammar to fit his new vocabularies, creating unexpected systems of meaning that we cannot decode in words, but that we intuit as fitting together like the solution to a puzzle, just as we may know by instinct that the hieroglyphs on an Egyptian building must make sense, even though we are unable to translate their message. It is worth mentioning that Salle admires the clashing imagery of the Irish poet Paul Muldoon, who specializes in simultaneously weaving together and disconnecting the commonplaces of our world.[2] Clearly, the time has come for artists and writers to make new kinds of order from new kinds of chaos.

1. David Salle in an interview with the author, *Artforum*, vol. XLI, no. 7 (March 2003), p. 264
2. *Ibid.* p. 75

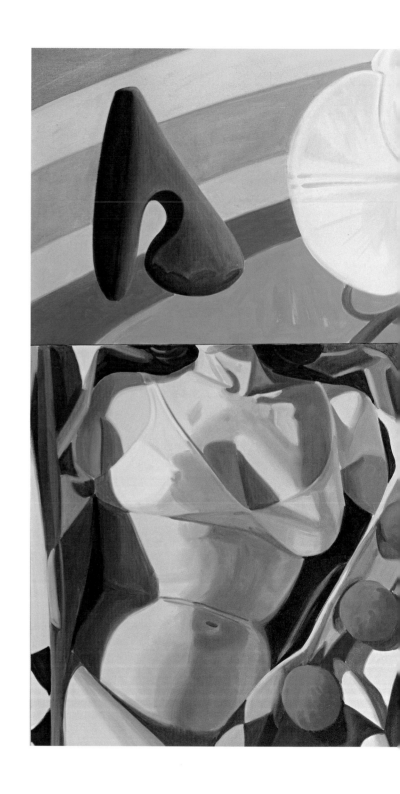

1.

Passers-by   2002

oil on linen

76 × 132 in / 193 × 335.3 cm

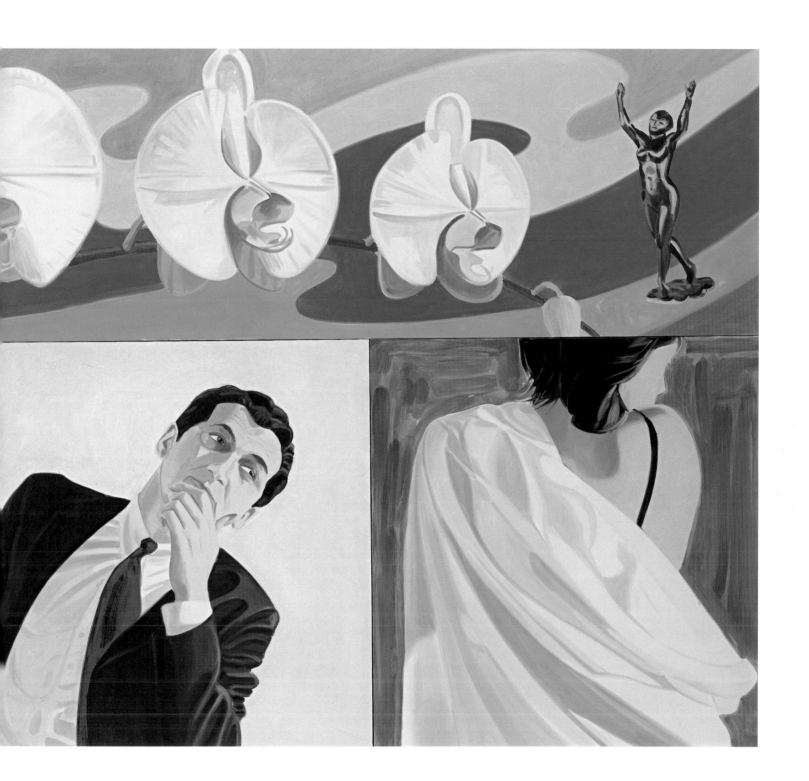

2.

Spill   2002

oil and acrylic on canvas and linen

78 ¼ × 84 in / 198.8 × 213.4 cm

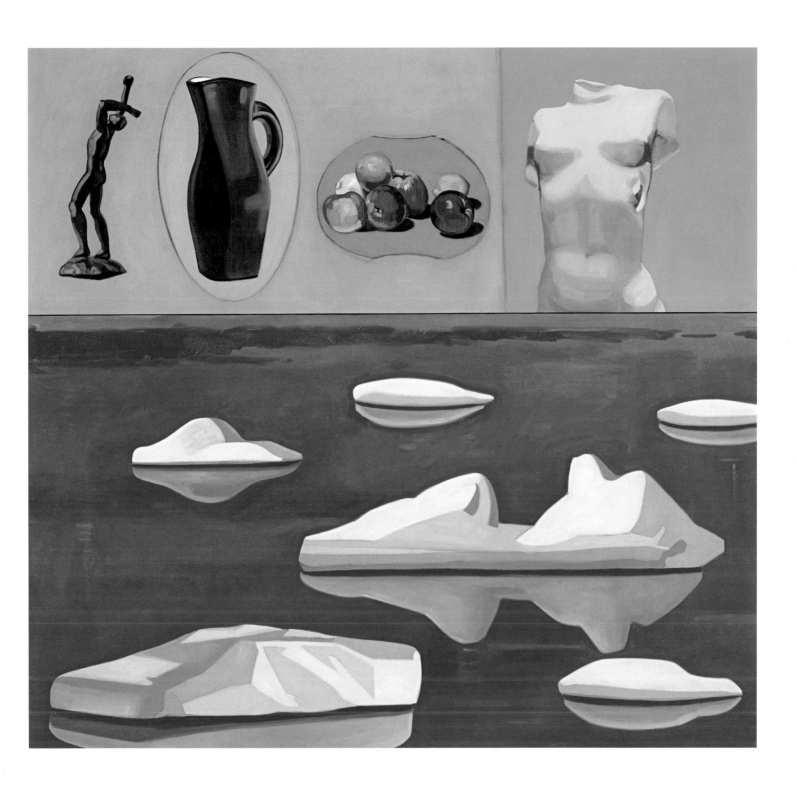

3.

Oxford Red   2003

oil on linen

18 × 27 ⅛ in / 45.7 × 68.9 cm

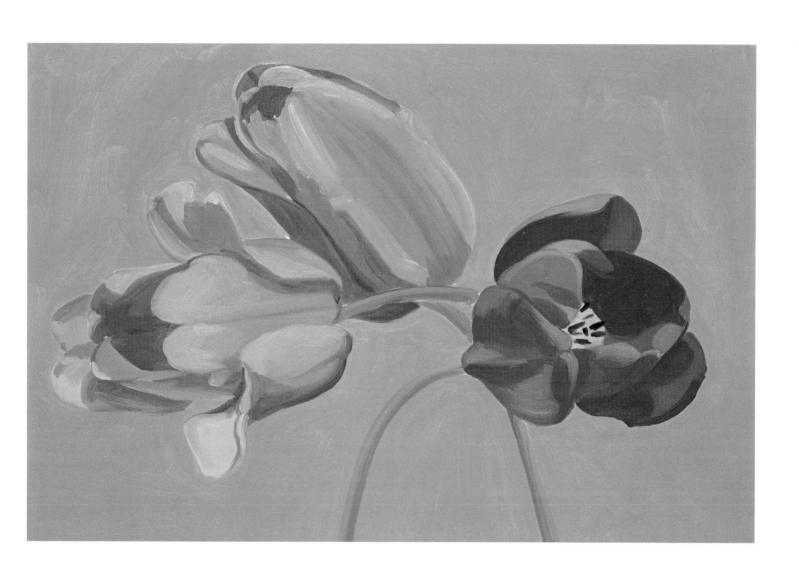

4.

Massimo with Daffodils   2003

oil on linen

35 ¾ × 24 ½ in / 90.8 × 62.2 cm

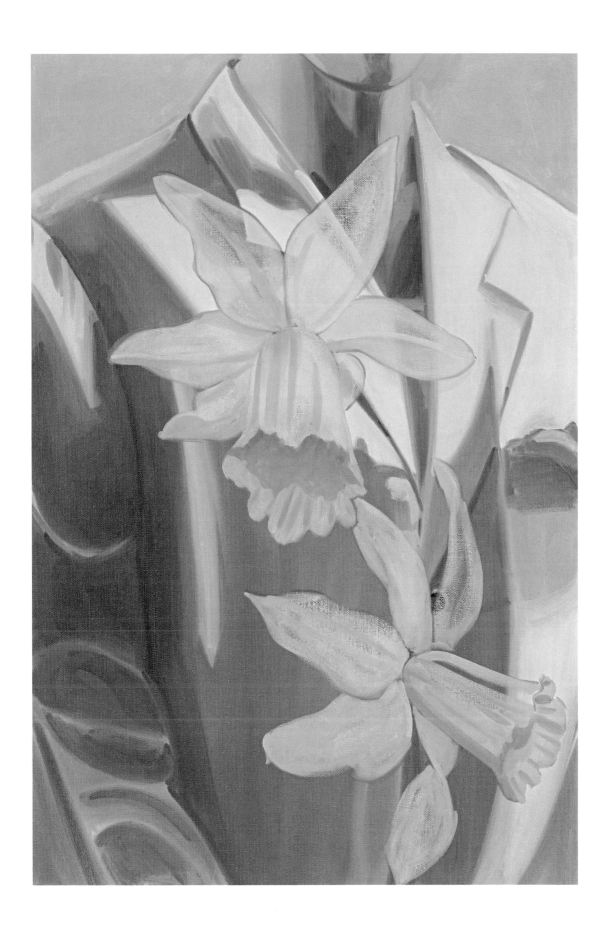

5.

Daffodils 2003

oil on linen

32 × 20 in / 81.3 × 50.8 cm

6.

Evaporation Machine   2003

oil on linen

84 × 84 in / 213.4 × 213.4 cm

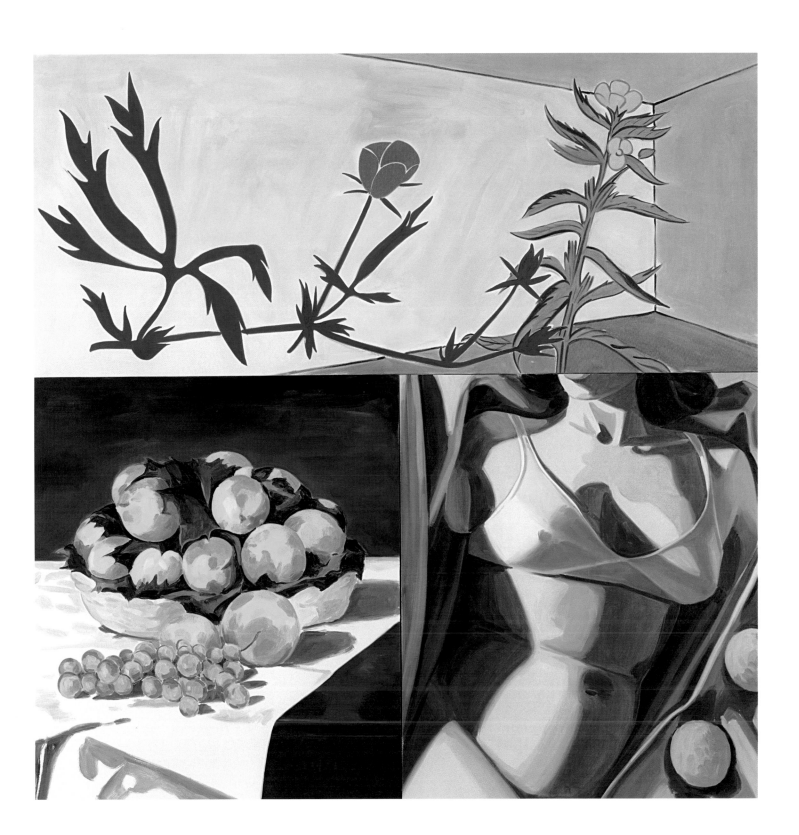

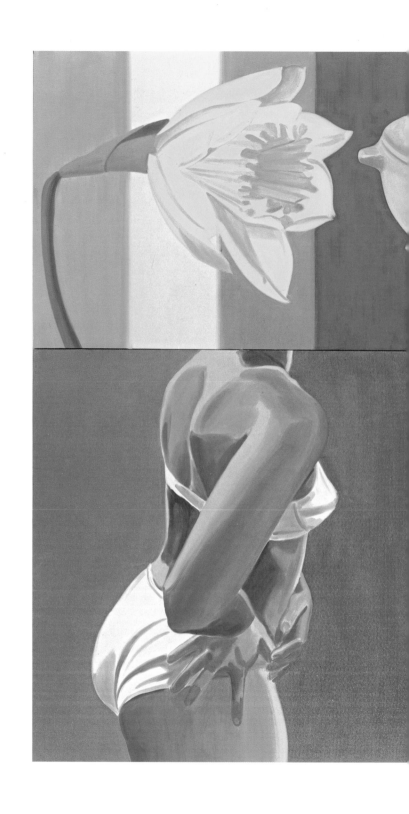

7.

Moraine   2003

oil on linen

76 × 132 in / 193 × 335.3 cm

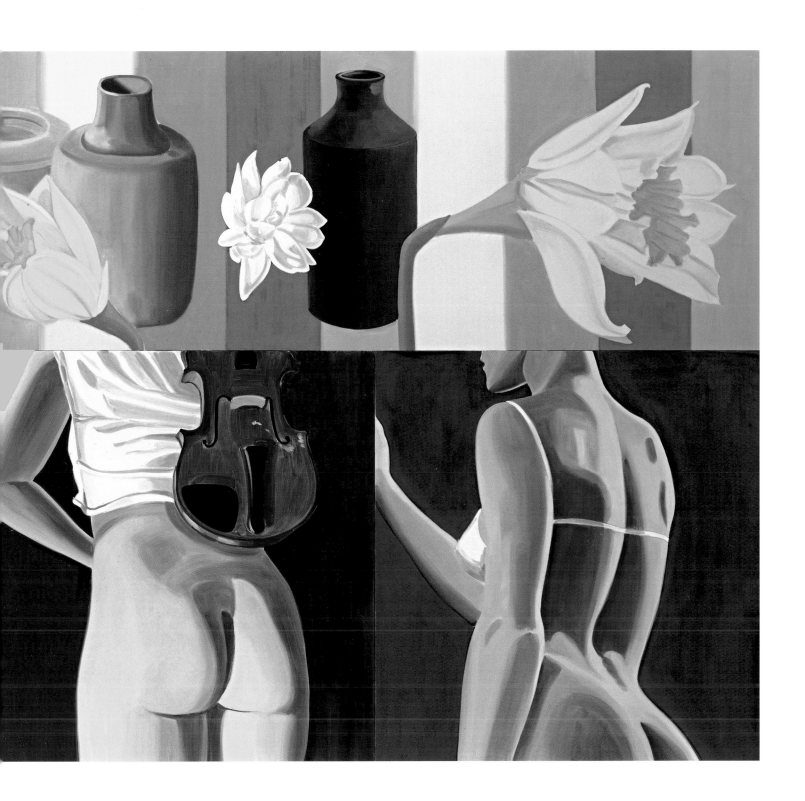

8.

Lemon Tree   2003

oil on linen

16 × 34 in / 40.6 × 86.4 cm

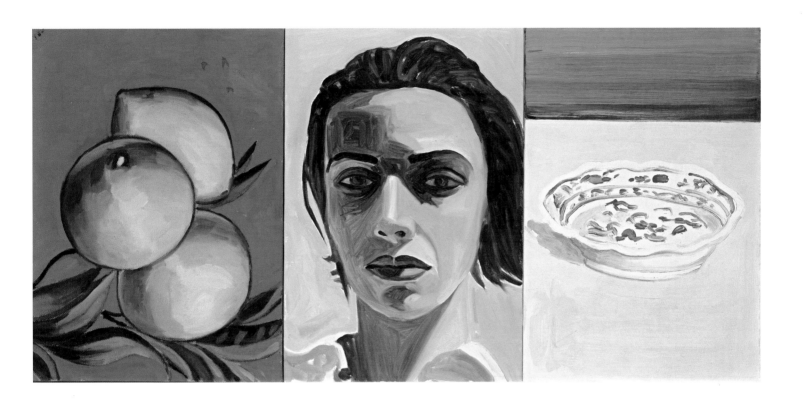

9.

Grey Felt Hat   2003

oil on linen

16 × 33 in / 40.6 × 83.8 cm

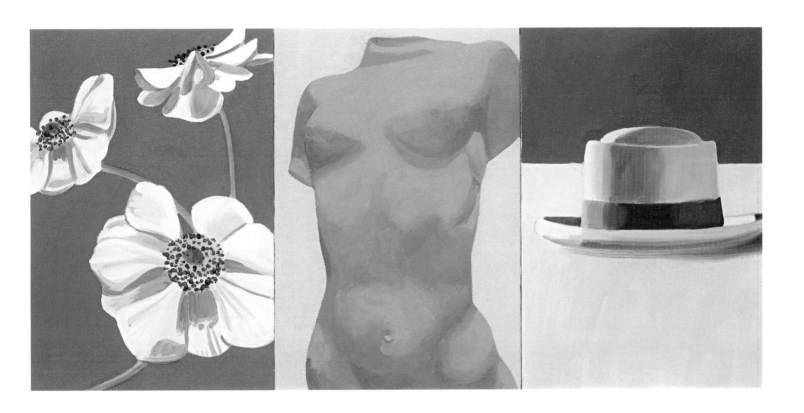

10.

Fall 2003

oil on linen

84 × 84 in / 213.4 × 213.4 cm

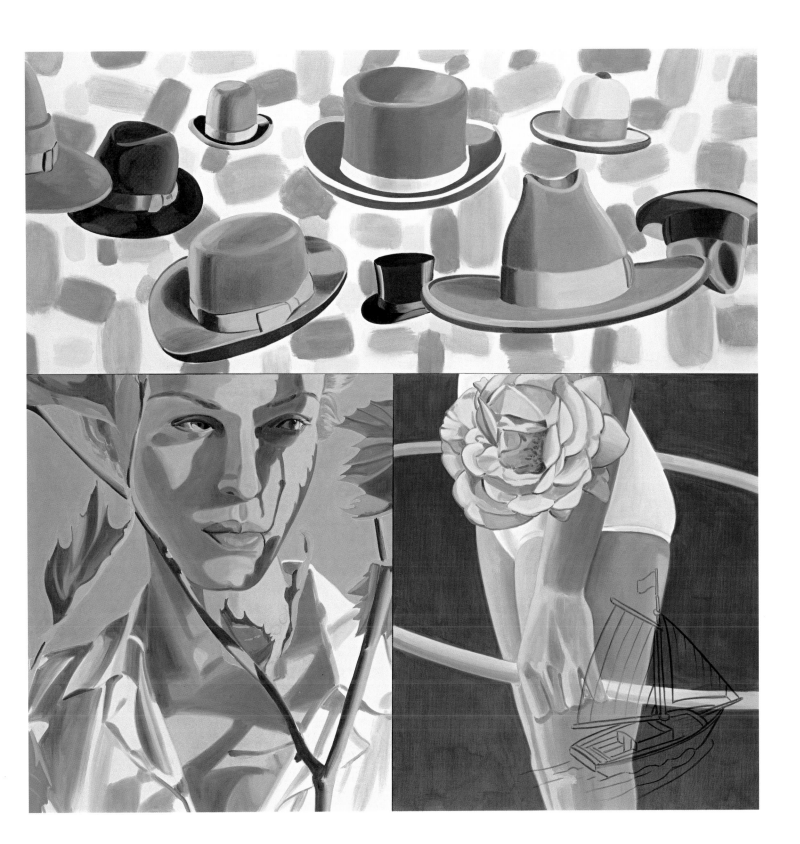

11.

150 Degrees   2003

oil on linen

80 × 88 in / 203.2 × 223.5 cm

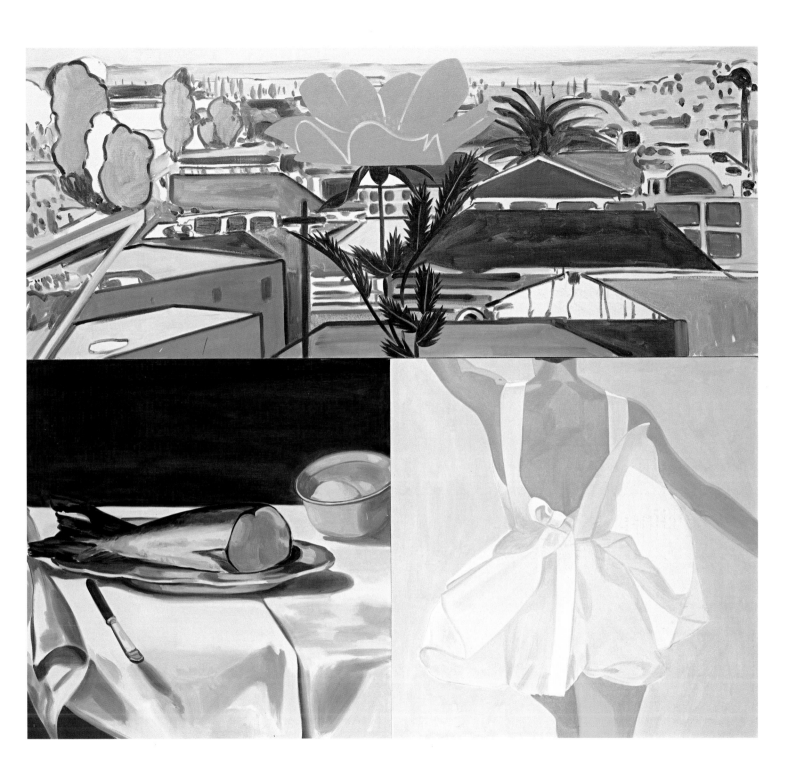

12.

Semi-Transparent Envelope   2003

oil on linen

76 × 76 in / 193 × 193 cm

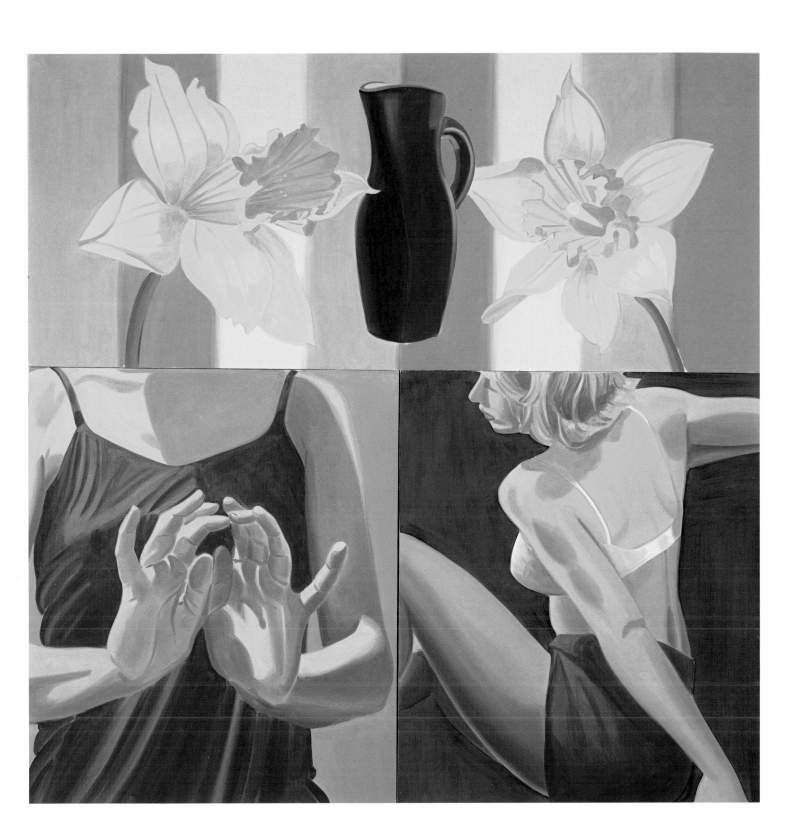

List of works

1. Passers-by 2002
oil on linen, 76 × 132 in / 193 × 335.3 cm

2. Spill 2002
oil and acrylic on canvas and linen, 78 ¼ × 84 in / 198.8 × 213.4 cm

3. Oxford Red 2003
oil on linen, 18 × 27 ⅛ in / 45.7 × 68.9 cm

4. Massimo with Daffodils 2003
oil on linen, 35 ¾ × 24 ½ in / 90.8 × 62.2 cm

5. Daffodils 2003
oil on linen, 32 × 20 in / 81.3 × 50.8 cm

6. Evaporation Machine 2003
oil on linen, 84 × 84 in / 213.4 × 213.4 cm

7. Moraine 2003
oil on linen, 76 × 132 in / 193 × 335.3 cm

8. Lemon Tree 2003
oil on linen, 16 × 34 in / 40.6 × 86.4 cm

9. Grey Felt Hat 2003
oil on linen, 16 × 33 in / 40.6 × 83.8 cm

10. Fall 2003
oil on linen, 84 × 84 in / 213.4 × 213.4 cm

11. 150 Degrees 2003
oil on linen, 80 × 88 in / 203.2 × 223.5 cm

12. Semi-Transparent Envelope 2003
oil on linen, 76 × 76 in / 193 × 193 cm

Biography

Born: 1952, Norman, Oklahoma
Education: 1973, BFA, California Institute of the Arts, Valencia, California; 1975, MFA, California Institute of the Arts, Valencia, California
Lives and works: Sagaponack, Long Island

SELECTED SOLO EXHIBITIONS

1976 Artists Space, New York
Foundation Corps de Garde, Groningen, The Netherlands

1977 *Bearding the Lion in His Den* (installation), Foundation de Appel, Amsterdam. Travelled to Foundation Corps de Garde, Groningen, The Netherlands; The Kitchen Center, New York

1979 Gagosian/Nosei-Weber Gallery, New York

1980 *Arti et Amicitiae*, Amsterdam (installation). Organised by Foundation de Appel, Amsterdam and Foundation Corps de Garde, Groningen
Neue Bilder, Galerie Bischofberger, Zürich

1981 Mary Boone Gallery, New York
Larry Gagosian Gallery, Los Angeles
Lucio Amelio Gallery, Naples

1982 *Man with a Camera*, Galleria Maria Diacono, Rome
Mary Boone Gallery/Leo Castelli Gallery, New York
Drawings, Galerie Bischofberger, Zürich
New Paintings, Anthony D'Offay Gallery, London

1983 *New Paintings*, Akira Ikeda Gallery, Tokyo
Mary Boone Gallery, New York
David Salle/Francis Picabia, Galerie Schellmann & Kluser, Munich
New Work, Ronald Greenberg Gallery, St Louis
Paintings, Museum Boymans-van Beuningen, Rotterdam
The Drunken Chauffeur: A Suite of 8 Screenprints, Castelli Graphics, New York
Neue Bilder und Aquarelle, Galerie Ascan Crone, Hamburg
New Paintings, Larry Gagosian Gallery, Los Angeles

1984 *Recent Paintings*, Leo Castelli Gallery, New York
Aquarelle, Galerie Bischofberger, Zürich
Galleria Mario Diacono, Rome
Neue Bilder, Galerie Bischofberger, Zürich

1985 Texas Gallery, Houston
Galerie Daniel Templon, Paris
Mary Boone Gallery, New York
Donald Young Gallery, Chicago
Galerie Bernard Kluser, Munich
Museum of Contemporary Art, Chicago
Sieben Bilder, Galerie Michael Werner, Cologne

1986 Leo Castelli Gallery, New York
Mario Diacono Gallery, Boston
Two New Suites of Prints, Castelli Graphics, New York
Works on Paper 1974-1986, Museum am Ostwall, Dortmund. Travelled to Aarhus Kunstmuseum, Aarhus, Denmark; The Institute of Contemporary Art, Boston

Institute of Contemporary Art, University of Pennsylvania, Philadelphia. Travelled to The Whitney Museum of American Art, New York; The Museum of Contemporary Art, Los Angeles; Art Gallery of Ontario, Toronto; Museum of Contemporary Art, Chicago
Galerie Bischofberger, Zürich

1987 *Il Teatro di David Salle: The Birth of a Poet*, Galleria di Franca Mancini, Pesaro, Italy
Mary Boone Gallery, New York
The Fruitmarket Gallery, Edinburgh
Galerie Bischofberger, Zürich
Spiral Garden, Wacoal Art Center, Tokyo

1988 *Recent Paintings*, Mary Boone/Michael Werner Gallery, New York
Two Noh Figures, Galerie Daniel Templon, Paris
The Menil Collection, Houston
Pinturas y acuarelas 1980-1988, Fundación Caja de Pensiones, Madrid. Travelled to the Staatsgalerie Modern Kunst, Munich; The Tel Aviv Museum of Art, Tel Aviv
New Paintings, Galerie Bischofberger, Zürich

1989 Waddington Galleries, London
Galerie Michael Werner, Cologne

1990 Waddington Graphics, London
Mario Diacono Gallery, Boston
Fred Hoffman Gallery, Santa Monica
Castelli Graphics, New York

1991 Gagosian Gallery, New York
Photographs, 1980-1990, Robert Miller Gallery, New York
American Social Dance, Galerie Bischofberger, Zürich

1992 Galerie Daniel Templon, Paris
David Salle Photographs, Stuart Regan Gallery, Los Angeles
Drawings, Gagosian Gallery, New York
Fantomas Series, Galerie Daniel Templon, Paris
Galeria Soledad Lorenzo, Madrid

1993 *New Paintings and Drawings*, Jason Rubell Gallery, Palm Beach
New Works, Newport Harbor Art Museum, California

1994 Mary Boone Gallery, New York
Gagosian Gallery, New York

1995 *Neue Bilder*, Galerie Bischofberger, Zürich
Tragedy, Comedy and Other New Paintings, Gagosian Gallery, New York

1996 *Obra 1995-1996*, Galeria Soledad Lorenzo, Madrid
New Works, Galerie Thaddaeus Ropac, Paris

1997 *New Paintings*, Gagosian Gallery, Beverly Hills
Galeria Soledad Lorenzo, Madrid
Maple Leaves, Claudia Gian Ferrari Arte Contemporanea, Milan

1998 *Recent Work*, Baldwin Gallery, Aspen
Itochu Gallery, Tokyo

1999 *Glass and Mirror Paintings*, Lehmann Maupin Gallery, New York
Bears / Interiors, Gagosian Gallery, New York

Retrospective, Stedelijk Museum, Amsterdam. Travelled to Museum Moderner Kunst Stiftung Ludwig, Vienna; Museo d'Arte Contemporanea Castello di Rivoli, Turin; Guggenheim Museum, Bilbao

2000   *Retrospective*, Museo de Arte Contemporáneo de Monterrey, A.C., Monterrey, Mexico
Dreams on Paper, Galleria In Arco, Turin

2001   *Pastorals*, Gagosian Gallery, New York
Jablonka Galerie, Cologne
Michael Lord Gallery, Milwaukee, Wisconsin

2002   Galleria Cardi, Milan
Lehmann Maupin Gallery, New York

2003   Mary Boone Gallery, New York

SPECIAL PROJECTS

THEATRE AND DANCE:

The Birth of a Poet, 1985, Director: Richard Foreman, Scenery and Costumes: David Salle, Brooklyn Academy of Music Next Wave Festival, New York

The Elizabethan Phrasing of the Late Albert Ayler, 1986, The Armitage Ballet, Choreography: Karole Armitage, Scenery and Costumes: David Salle, Eindhoven, Holland

The Mollino Room, 1986, The American Ballet Theatre, Choreography: Karole Armitage, Scenery and Costumes: David Salle, The Kennedy Center for the Performing Arts, Washington DC

Tarnished Angels, 1987, The Paris Opera Ballet, Choreography: Karole Armitage, Design: David Salle, Costumes: Christian Lacroix, Paris

Contempt, 1989, The Armitage Ballet, Choreography: Karole Armitage, Scenery and Costumes: David Salle with Jeff Koons, Opera Comique, Paris

FEATURE FILM:

Search and Destroy, 1994-1995,
Director: David Salle, Producer: Martin Scorsese

AWARDS

Guggenheim Fellowship for theatre design, awarded 1986

COMMISSIONS

1996   *Crystal River*, Nagahori Project, Osaka, Japan, large public space
1997   *Songs for Sale*, Key Tower, Cleveland, Ohio, office building
1998   Daimler Chrysler Corporation, Berlin, Architect: Renzo Piano, corporate headquarters
1999   The Mattel Corporation, Los Angeles, corporate headquarters

PUBLIC COLLECTIONS

Addison Gallery of American Art, Andover, Massachusetts
Akron Art Museum
Art Enterprise LTD/Kanter Family Collection, Chicago
Art Institute of Chicago
Bard College/Marieluise Hessel Collection, New York
Eli Broad Family Foundation, Los Angeles
Carnegie Institute, Pittsburgh
Chase Manhattan Collection, New York
Chicago Museum of Contemporary Art
The Cleveland Museum of Art
Douglas S. Cramer Foundation, Los Angeles
Davidson Art Center, Middletown, Connecticut
Essl Collection, Klosterneuburg/Vienna
Guild Hall, East Hampton, New York
The Solomon R. Guggenheim Museum, New York
Ho-Am Museum, Seoul
Israel Museum, Jerusalem
Kunstmuseum, Basel
Los Angeles County Museum of Art
Louisiana Museum of Art, Humlebaek, Denmark
Ludwig Forum für International Kunst, Cologne
Metropolitan Museum of Art, New York
Milwaukee Art Museum
Museum Boymans-van Beuningen, Rotterdam
Museum of Contemporary Art, Los Angeles
Musée National D'Art Moderne, Centre Georges Pompidou, Paris
The Museum of Modern Art, New York
Nationalgalerie, Berlin
National Gallery, Washington DC
Nelson-Atkins Museum of Art, Kansas City
The New York Public Library
North Carolina Museum of Art, Raleigh, North Carolina
Norton Simon Museum, Pasadena
The Paine Webber Collection, New York
The Parish Art Museum, Southampton, New York
Portland Art Museum
Rubell Family Collection, Miami
Saatchi Gallery, London
San Francisco Museum of Modern Art
Sintra Museum of Modern Art, Portugal
Stedelijk Museum, Amsterdam
Stedelijk Van Abbe Museum, Eindhoven
Tacoma Art Museum
Tate, London
University of Michigan Museum of Art, Ann Arbor
Virginia Museum of Fine Arts, Richmond, Virginia
Wichita Art Museum
Whitney Museum of American Art, New York
Yale University Art Gallery, New Haven, Connecticut

SELECTED BIBLIOGRAPHY

MONOGRAPHS:

1986 *David Salle*, texts by Janet Kardon and Lisa Liebmann, Institute of Contemporary Art, Philadelphia
David Salle, texts by Robert Rosenblum and Rainer Crone, translation by Michael Lipson and Dennis Cooper, Galerie Bischofberger, Zürich

1989 *Karole Armitage and David Salle: 3 Years of the Ballet Stage*, text by Peter Schjeldahl, Kyoto Shoin International Co. Ltd, Kyoto

1994 *David Salle*, editor: David Whitney, text by Lisa Liebmann, Rizzoli International Publications, New York

1999 *David Salle: Retrospective*, texts by Rudi Fuchs, Dorine Mignot, and Frederic Tuten, Stedelijk Museum/Ludion, Ghent/Amsterdam (additional printings in German, Spanish, Italian)

2000 *David Salle: Retrospective*, texts by Xavier López de Arriaga, Walter Hopps, and Molly Nesbit, Museo de Arte Contemporáneo de Monterrey, A.C., Monterrey, Mexico

2002 *David Salle: Immediate Experience*, editor: Sarah French, texts by Wayne Koestenbaum and Mimmo Paladino, Gabrius SpA, Milan

EXHIBITION CATALOGUES:

1982 *David Salle: Man with a Camera*, text by Mario Diacono, Galleria Mario Diacono, Rome

1983 *David Salle: Neue Bilder und Aquarelle*, text by Michael Kruger, Galerie Ascan Crone, Hamburg
David Salle: Paintings, texts by W.A.L. Beeren and Carter Ratcliff, Museum Boymans-van Beuningen, Rotterdam
David Salle, Francis Picabia, text by Ingrid Rein, Verlag Schellmann & Kluser, Munich
David Salle, Akira Ikeda Gallery, Tokyo

1984 *David Salle: Imagine Totale*, text by Mario Diacono, Galleria Mario Diacono, Rome

1985 *David Salle*, text by John Hawkes, Mary Boone/Michael Werner Gallery, New York
David Salle: Sieben Bilder, text by Peter Schjeldahl, Galerie Michael Werner, Cologne

1986 *David Salle: Works on Paper 1974-1986*, text by Ernst A. Busche, Museum Am Ostwall, Dortmund
David Salle, text by Dennis Cooper, Galerie Bischofberger, Zürich
David Salle, text by Mario Diacono, Mario Diacono Gallery, Boston

1987 *David Salle*, text by Junhi Itoh, Wacoal Art Center, Tokyo
David Salle, text by Peter Schjeldahl, Elizabeth Avedon Editions/Vintage Contemporary Artists, New York
David Salle, text by Richard Thomson, The Fruitmarket Gallery, Edinburgh
David Salle: The Birth of a Poet, Rossini Opera Festival: Galleria di Franca Mancini, Pesaro

1988 *David Salle*, text by Frederic Tuten, Mary Boone/Michael Werner Gallery, New York

1989 *David Salle*, text by Dan Cameron, Waddington Galleries, London
David Salle, text by Wilfried Dickhoff, Galerie Michael Werner, Cologne
David Salle, texts by Kevin Power and Carla Schulz-Hoffman, Fundación Caja de Pensiones, Madrid

1990 *David Salle*, text by Mario Diacono, Mario Diacono Gallery, Boston
David Salle: Canfield Hatfield 1989-1990, A Series of Nine Etchings and Aquatints, Waddington Graphics, London

1991 *David Salle: American Social Dance*, Galerie Bischofberger, Zürich
David Salle: Photographs, text by Henry Geldzahler, edited and designed by John Cheim, Robert Miller Gallery, New York
David Salle, text by Fréderique Lucien, Galerie Nationale du Jeu de Paume, Paris
David Salle, text by George W.S. Trow, Gagosian Gallery, New York

1992 *David Salle: Drawings*, text by Rudi Fuchs, Gagosian Gallery, New York
David Salle, text by Kevin Power, translation by Javier Torre, Galeria Soledad Lorenzo, Madrid

1994 *Early Product Paintings*, text by Diego Cortez, Gagosian Gallery, New York

1996 *David Salle*, text by Rosa Olivares, translation by Francisco Javier Torre Ribelles, Galeria Soledad Lorenzo, Madrid
David Salle: Malerei: Ein Kunstwissenschaftlicher Meta-Ansatz, text by Rudiger Kogel, Jahn & Ernst Verlag, Hamburg

1997 *David Salle: Maple Leaves*, text by Massimo Audiello, Galleria Gian Ferrari, Milan

1998 *David Salle*, text by Akira Tatehata, translation by Mari Saegusa, Itochu Gallery, Tokyo
David Salle: The 80's, text by Maria De Corral, Culturgest, Lisbon
David Salle, text by Sergio Risaliti, Piazza Del Plebiscito, Naples

1999 *David Salle: Retrospective*, text by Arjen Mulder, Ludion, Ghent/Amsterdam
David Salle: Bears/Interiors, text by Hilton Als, Gagosian Gallery, New York
David Salle: Glass and Mirror Paintings, text by Molly Nesbit, Lehmann Maupin Gallery, New York
Phillips, Lisa, *The American Century: Art & Culture, 1950-2000 Part 2*, Whitney Museum of American Art, New York
20 Years/20 Artists, text by Farver Suzanne, Aspen Art Museum, Colorado
David Salle Retrospective, text by Frederic Tuten, Ludion, Ghent/Amsterdam

2000 *David Salle: Dreams on Paper*, text by Luca Beatrice, Galleria In Arco, Turin

2001 *David Salle: Pastoral*, text by Ronald Jones, Gagosian Gallery, New York
David Salle: Ice Flow, text by Robert Hullot-Kentor, Jablonka Galerie, Cologne

2002 de Pury, Simon, *Ahead of the 21st Century the Pisces Collection*, Hatje Cantz Publishers, Germany
Some Assembly Required: Collage Culture in Post-War America, Syracuse/Everson Museum of Art, New York

2003 Coen, Vittoria, *Pictura Magistra Vitae, I nuovi simboli della pittura contemporanea (The new symbols of contemporary painting)*, Fondazione Cassa Di Risparmio, Bologna

The Directors of Waddington Galleries would like to thank David Salle
and Mary Schwab for their generous help in organising the exhibition

David Salle
17 September – 11 October 2003

Waddington Galleries
11 Cork Street
London
W1S 3LT

Telephone + 44 20 7851 2200 / 020 7851 2200
Facsimile + 44 20 7734 4146 / 020 7734 4146

mail@waddington-galleries.com
www.waddington-galleries.com

Monday – Friday 10am – 5.30pm
Saturday 10.30am – 1.30pm

Photography by Prudence Cuming Associates Ltd
except cat. no.2 by Robert McKeever
and cat. no.12 by Zindman/Fremont
Designed and typeset by Peter Campbell, London
Printed by PJ Print, London

© David Salle 2003
© Robert Rosenblum 2003
© Waddington Galleries 2003

Published by Waddington Galleries

ISBN 0-9545441-1-0

Cover: detail from *Evaporation Machine* 2003 (cat. no.6)